John
Thank you!

IRAQ IN PICTURES

as seen from the eyes of soldiers

COMPILED AND WRITTEN BY PHIL KIVER

Printed in the United States of America.

ISBN: 978 1 59571 286 8

Library of Congress Control Number: 2001012335

Designed and Published by:
Word Association Publishers
205 Fifth Avenue
Tarentum, Pennsylvania 15084

www.wordassociation.com
1.800.827.7903

Iraq in Pictures is a compilation of the following photographic contributions:
• Author, Phil Kiver (photos taken 2004-2005)
• SPC L.B. Edgar (photos taken 2007-2008)
• Various soldiers, Courtesy of U.S. Army and Department of Defense Public Affairs

Book Design: Gina Datres, Word Association Publishers

DEDICATED TO

MY DAUGHTER

ADDISON HERO

FOREWORD

by Major General (Ret) Tom Matthews

It seems that all day every day we are afforded opportunities to see, hear, and read about who we are fighting against in Iraq. Phil Kiver, in his captivating collection of photographs shows who we are fighting for in Iraq. Phil shows the other side of the story, the people of Iraq, the children, moms, dads and ordinary everyday citizens. He also shows the rest of the story—the soldiers, Marines, allies, coalition partners, contractors and Iraqis who are sacrificing and working to secure the victory.

More so than words ever could, the pictures show the stories behind the stories:

- The contrast between the palaces and wealth of Saddam against the poverty and failed infrastructure of Iraq.
- The good times of the brotherhood of soldiers and their worst of times and living conditions.
- The vast array of allies and coalition partners working as one to transition to a stable Iraq.

- The rich history and culture of Iraq and the contrast with the culture of the West.
- The efforts at reconciliation and an American example of the rule of law.
- The Iraqi people trying to live normal and ordinary lives under a constant threat of terrorist activity.
- The Soldiers from around the world serving as role models of democracy for the people of Iraq.

For several years, a constant theme in the press was that America was "going it alone in Iraq". During a coalition planning conference in Poland, military leaders from numerous countries told me how offended they were with the perception created by the media that America was "going it alone in Iraq". One military leader from a very small country told me that one half of his military was serving in Iraq. While it was a small force he said that his countries contribution relative to their size was substantial. The challenge and complexity of securing a victory are shown in every picture of this book. Phil shows we are not "going it alone in Iraq". Pictures throughout the book show the courage and commitment of our soldiers, allies, and coalition partners. Phil's pictures show soldiers from a vast array of nations—Australia, Bulgaria, Canada, Estonia, Italy, Kazakhstan, Mongolia, and Romania supporting the people of Iraq. It is important to note that these pictures are not all-inclusive of the many nations involved in this mission.

Reconciliation is one of the pillars of post conflict recovery. Implementing the rule of law is critical to ensure a fair, just, and non-lethal process exists to resole conflict and provide closure for crimes and inhumanities that has taken place. The pictures of Saddam are part of the story of reconciliation and justice to many in Iraq. The inclusion of the Abu Ghraib sketches is a difficult thing for any soldier to deal with. It is sad but it is also important. It demonstrates that soldiers are held to a higher standard. It also shows that the rule of law applies to everyone. The reason our military is so respected today is that no one is harder on us than we are on ourselves.

At the conclusion of major combat operations in Iraq the slow restoration of infrastructure and utilities received a good deal of media attention. Many of Phil's pictures show the real challenge faced in Iraq. That challenge was not in repairing infrastructure damaged during the conflict. It was building or rebuilding infrastructure that Saddam had let deteriorate beyond repair. Phil's pictures show that in Saddam's Iraq, palaces and personal wealth were significantly more important than quality of life for Iraqis.

The art of war is 2,000 years old. The courageous individuals in Phil's pictures are defining the Art of Peace. The Soldiers, Sailors, Airmen and Marines with boots on the ground who are serving in dangerous and austere conditions. Only a soldier can understand the challenge of maintaining a passion for fighting insurgents while demonstrating compassion for the populace. Picture after picture shows extraordinary examples of our American military values in providing medical treatment to an insurgent, compassion to children and adults and tireless efforts to build quality of life for Iraqis. There is a trite phrase dating back to the Vietnam era, "Winning the hearts and minds of the people". As shown in his pictures chronicling the efforts of the military, they are not about the work of "Winning hearts and minds". They are about the work of "Earning hearts and minds". Despite all of the transformation and technology of the military, securing the victory is still done the old fashioned, low-tech, no-tech, one-child, one-family, one village at a time. It is each individual soldier serving as a role model representative of a democratic nation, living the core values of the military.

As soldiers serve throughout the world, they quickly realize that we live in the Promised Land. They also realize that we can't bring everyone to the Promised Land. At best, all we can give others, like the people of Iraq, is a chance to build what we have. Our young soldiers today are giving the people of Iraq a window of time and role model examples to build what we often take for granted. Having never lived in a true democracy, it may be a long time before they fully comprehend the gift our soldiers have given them.

In a world rapidly becoming homogenous, Phil Kiver shows that Iraq, for better or worse, has escaped that phenomenon. Picture after picture shows an ancient world of culture, beliefs and infrastructure existing in parallel with the high technology, diverse culture and Western values of the coalition forces. The sharpest contrast is shown in the many pictures of our female soldiers serving in Iraq and in their interaction with the women of Iraq.

Phil concludes the book with a chapter on progress. For the two parallel universes of Iraq, change is relative. The people of the region view the progress and change (637 to 2003 versus 2003 to 2008) as revolutionary, dramatic and traumatic. For the West, change and progress has been slow, tedious and costly in lives and national treasure. The insurgents in Iraq have a saying, "The Americans have all of the watches in the world and we have all of the time in the world." Only history will show if the patience of the Middle Eastern culture will win out against the impatience of the Western culture.

Oone day while looking over my personal collection of books, I noticed how many picture books featuring the American Civil War were on my bookshelves. Books of various sizes, many with same photographs. This led me to the idea of putting together a picture book of my own on the current war in Iraq. I went through the thousands of photos that I had from my tour as well as those contributed by friends and other soldiers.

Thus *Iraq in Pictures* was born.

The author, Phil Kiver and his daughter Addison

My intent for this book was twofold: first to preserve for history the images of this war so that 147 years from now, military historians and students will look at their bookshelves and find the Iraq war in photographs. Second: I wanted civilians to see what the soldier sees and how the soldiers of this conflict lived and died. For too long, newspapers both for and against this war have presented photos of the war taken out of context, with bias presented as fact.

I also hope this book will encourage other veterans to release their photos and preserve for history, the many years of conflict we have gone through since 9-11. Some of the photos in *Iraq in Pictures* are graphic and shocking; others are heartwarming. Either way, my goal has been to expand your view and understanding of the war as a whole as you witness how the soldiers, marines, airmen, and others functioned in this austere and dangerous environment.

When I speak about my strong support for the war, I always ask how anyone could deny the opportunity for freedom to the children of Iraq or to those anywhere else in the world? I believe Americans have a moral obligation to help oppressed people. Our blessings of freedom and liberty should be afforded to all nations and people. If that means going after a dictator or terrorist leader, so be it. As a soldier, I felt it was a privilege to help others win their freedom. We must support our leaders and military when the cause is the expansion of freedom and democracy.

As you study the photos of the children in this book, be proud of the special care our soldiers have taken to reach out to the children of Iraq—those who have not yet been taught to hate—whose smiles made it possible for soldiers to get through another day of violence and fear. We take so much for granted in America, that it is difficult to understand how a toy or a piece of candy can accomplish more in ten seconds than all of the meetings and wars have done or will ever do.

As always I extend my deepest gratitude to those who support the military and what they do for all America's and the rest of the world.

Please enjoy the photos!

I once attended the funeral of a soldier in Arlington National Cemetery. An Iraq veteran myself, it was something I wanted to witness. It was important to me to get past the tourist track of the cemetery. As I walked behind the soldiers and horse-drawn caisson my emotions were torn. I had deep pride for those in the military who gave their lives and I felt rage at those protesters who would deny a soldier's right to die for the freedoms of others. How dare anyone think he or she knows better than these brave soldiers who serve with such distinction. In a world short

I believe sharing and sacrificing for others is the American way.

on heroes, I recommend a trip to Arlington. You don't have to know the Seamen, Airmen, Marine or Soldier remembered there. I didn't personally know First LT Mark Dooley from Vermont, except for the fact that he is a true American hero.

TABLE OF CONTENTS

1

LIVING CONDITIONS OF SOLDIERS

One of Saddam's palaces on the water that was bombed out over the years. Saddam had 67 palaces in a country the size of California. All of them had pools and air conditioning with gold fixtures. Most people do not realize how much wealth he had while his people suffered under horrible living conditions. How much wealth does one dictator need?

An Iraqi bat house. One of the strangest sights in Iraq. The bats were welcome friends to keep the problem of malaria to a minimum.

Outside view of the Post Exchange or PX. Large concrete barricades are to stop car bombers and anyone else from trying to harm those inside. ID cards have to be shown for anyone to enter the building. This is where soldiers can go and purchase the things they needed such as razors and DVDs. The popular items go very fast. If you want to help a soldier, send him or her AA batteries or sunglasses. Both are very important.

This is a group of all of the senior leadership of our allies at Christmas time. At the time of this photo, over 26 other nations had troops in Iraq. It was never just the United States and Britain, as the media portrays.

Outside view of mess hall. These conrete barriers are meant to prevent car bombers. In addition, everyone has to show ID cards to an armed U. S. soldier at the door. I even had to take a turn performing guard duty for a day. As you can see, there is no overhead protection from incoming indirect fire, but we did the best we could with what we had. All soldiers take their weapons with them everywhere they go. Halliburton fed us well!

Left: This what the inside of most bathroom trailers look like when cleaned. Most of the time they are dirty with soldiers washing off the dust and sweat of war. Just being able to sit and relax after a shower, and maybe put on a clean pair of socks was very special after a day-long mission.

Below: The all-important gym, complete with music and TV. Many soldiers, when not working, spend all of their free time here. The roof is just a tent. Luckily no mortar or rockets hit while I was stationed at this camp.

Chow being served to the troops by the officers on Thanksgiving Day. We had everything to eat that you could possibly hope to get at home. Notice that officers are serving the enlisted soldiers. This is a Boxing Day tradition picked up from the British Army, in which enlisted and officers switch places for a day. My friend and I went to get food supplies from the mess hall and had a feast of our own. I was able to eat with soldiers from 13 other nations at one time for my Thanksgiving celebration.

Burger King! Need I say more? What a wonderful treat this was for many soldiers far from home—to be able to have it "their way." Sometimes, something as simple as a Whopper can help a homesick soldier.

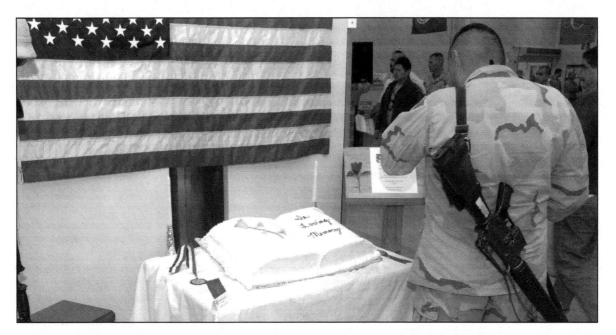

This is a memorial in the mess hall to a fallen soldier. The Department of Defense does not think we should show photos of coffins with flags on them. I disagree. Americans need to know the sacrifices and the costs. We see cemeteries. What do you think is in the ground? I do not want soldiers' names to be broadcast; however, we need to see, so when the number hits 5,000 or 6,000 or higher, we are not shocked.

This is the dessert bar in one of our mess halls. To be honest, I never ate the dessert. I always thought of soldiers in past wars who never had it so good. I actually told some people off who I thought were abusing this privilege—compared to veterans of other conflicts.

One of the living areas after a rain storm in the Baghdad area. People don't think of Iraq as a wet place, but there is a wet season. It was either hot or wet all of the time. Rain in the desert makes mud, which is why the gravel was put down. The mud sticks to everything, including itself and your boots.

Right: Outside view of living trailers. These two-room units sleep four people most of the time. I stayed in a tent the entire six months I was in Iraq.

Bottom: Soldier playing a game of bean bag toss with the locals. Some things are the same no matter where you go in the world.

Saddam's palace at Camp Victory. This compound was built by Saddam as a hunting reserve for him and his buddies. He had exotic animals imported from all over the world. The moat was filled with fish to catch. Every now and then, we would see or capture an animal like a cheetah or gazelle that had no business living in Iraq. What an absolute waste of money! While his people suffered, Saddam spent his time killing animals for sport.

Above: Soldiers enjoying the little bit of shade they can find.

Right: Master Sgt. Jaan Soosalu, an assistant platoon sergeant with Estonian Platoon 15, which works with Troop B, 1st Squadron, 7th Cavalry Regiment, 1st Brigade Combat Team, 1st Cavalry Division, looks for hidden weapons in Saba al Bor, a town on the northern outskirts of Baghdad Province, during a search of a predominantly Shia neighborhood. The Estonian soldiers searched abandoned buildings and residents' homes for unauthorized weapons, explosives and signs of criminal-militia operations. (U.S. Army photo by Spc. L.B. Edgar, 7th Mobile Public Affairs Detachment.)

Melbourne, Arkansas native SPC Matthew Yancey, a team leader with Company C, 1st Battalion, 64th Armor Regiment, 2nd Brigade Combat Team, 3rd Infantry Division, finishes a bottle of water during a patrol in western Baghdad. Over the course of the mission, Yancey and the soldiers with his team drank several bottles of water each day to stay hydrated in spite of the extreme heat. (U.S. Army photo by SPC L.B. Edgar, 7th Mobile Public Affairs Detachment.)

Lawndale, North Carolina native PFC Kevin Johnson, an infantryman with 1st Platoon, Company C, 2nd Battalion, 325th Airborne Infantry Regiment, 2nd Brigade Combat Team, 82nd Airborne Division, walks through Ur, a neighborhood within Baghdad's Adhamiyah District. The paratroopers went door-to-door to gather information from residents who were being terrorized by criminal militia. (U.S. Army photo by SPC L.B. Edgar, 7th Mobile Public Affairs Detachment.)

EQUIPMENT

Above: 155 Howitzer firing in the battle of Fallujah. Manning the guns are Marine reservists from northern Georgia and Tennessee. For part-timers these guys sure knew their guns. I was able to pull the lanyard and fire this gun as well.

Right: Pilot in front of his Apache Attack Chopper.

Marine mechanic on chopper. Everyone has a job to do in order to accomplish the mission. For every combat soldier, there are two or three others to support him, as this Marine mechanic is doing. This is one of the principal reasons we have so many soldiers deployed at any given time. Someone has to be there to turn the wrench, sort the mail, and deliver the gasoline.

Left: Italian soldier learning to fire one of the terrorists' favorite weapons, the rocket propelled grenade.

Below: Soviet-made tank. These are what the new Iraqi Army is playing with now, plenty of spare parts to be found all over the world. We can kill these tanks with ours before they even know we are there.

While the AK-47 may be salvaged, the human leg next to it has definitely seen better days. These are the types of photos people need to see, as conflicts continue around the world. War is not clean. Even air campaigns, like the one in the Balkans, lead to death and devastation.

Italian tanks and chopper at a base in southern Iraq. Italy is and has been an important partner in the war on terror and in Iraq as well.

Right: American tank kicks up ever-present dust in the streets of Baghdad. These large vehicles make inviting targets for car bombers.

Below: UH-60 Black Hawk, my primary transportaion while in Iraq.

Chevy pickup gives all my Italian friends a ride in Iraq. I am on the left on the tailgate with SPC Franks, on the right.

Utah and Texas combat engineer soldiers pulling guard duty and supervision of a highway construction project in southern Iraq. Progress and construction have been ongoing for most of the time since 2003.

Right: Iraqi Highway Patrol pose with their weapons. In the southern region of Iraq, life is fairly quiet, and they only deal with bandits and thieves.

Below: A Romanian practicing with a sniper rifle at gun range.

A beautiful day in Karbala, in southern Iraq

Italian Army work dogs. I wonder if they bark in Italian—just as the Iraqi cats meow in Arabic.

Another Italian Army work dog. Dogs are a very important part of the mission in Iraq. They sniff for bombs, guard prisoners, and in some cases, save their masters' lives. Not to be forgotten, they have on more than a few occasions become part of the list of the fallen.

U.S. dump truck helps out with hauling gravel for the highway. Truck driven by Utah National Guard soldiers, proving you really can do any job in the Army!

3

FOOD & DRINK

A picture-perfect Italian meal, ready to be served. General Depascale, Italian Forces, on the left; Colonel Herrington, USMC from Arkansas on the right—both very good friends of mine.

Left: Here I am eating some lamb and rice which was made by soldiers from Kazakhstan. One of the things I enjoyed most while in Iraq was experiencing other cultures.

Below: I am sad in the photo because I ran out of sour cream & onion potato chips. They were hard to find and did not survive the mail well at all. When I found them, I ate them very fast.

A traditional meal,
fresh goat, is often
served by the Iraqis as
a show of hospitality.

FRIENDS/FELLOW SOLDIERS

4

Headquaters Company III Corps Warriors. All of these soldiers are from Fort Hood, Texas. I love these kinds of photos because they really show the bond between soldiers—as they have seen it all together and lived to tell the tale.

Left: LTG Thomas Metz, Multi National Corps Commander, pictured with a soldier who just became a U.S. citizen. Metz presided over the naturalization ceremony in Al-Faw Palace, where many service members became U.S. citizens.

Below: Two out of two Iraqis agree: John Kerry was not for them or America.

A different place—a different culture. Four women take time to interact with one another, including the female soldier holding the baby.

I pledge allegiance...
Spc. Dima, on left, was killed one week after taking his oath as a U.S. citizen at this naturalization ceremony in Baghdad.

Above: LTC John Reed III, Corps chaplain, gives the invocation for the naturalization ceremony.

Right: Major Monger, Utah National Guard Engineer Officer, confers with local Interior official.

Mongolian soldiers on right and left. Kazakhstan soldier in the middle.

Major General Weber United States Marine Corps and General DePascale Italian Forces, were the best of friends. This kind of close partnership is essential in the new war on terror.

Left: My good friend, Antonio Italian non-commissioned officer, with his pirate look.

Below: Antonio with his Romeo looks and actions. He was the perfect diplomat, here asking for a light from a U.S. Marine.

Right: SPC Kevin Franks gives his best warrior look for the camera. I am below left. Franks is on the right. He was my friend and confidant in Iraq.

Below: Here I am all suited up while filming on the highway in southern Iraq. I know I look stupid in those glasses but the ballistic eyewear saved my eyes on one occasion.

Left: PFC Bigenho, an army journalist stops to jot down some quick notes on her pad so she can write an article when she returns to camp.

Below: Bulgarian soldier and I after he insisted on a photo with me. I got the blue patch on his uniform though so it was all worth it. His unit had the patches specially made to denote their service in Iraq. A few seconds under my pocket knife, and that sucker was mine. I did give him an American flag patch in return, so our relations are still very good. This kind of swapping has been going on since units began receiving individual patches in the American Civil War. I collected as many countries and units as I could.

Above: Air Force Senior Non Commissioned Officer and a young Army Captain exchange mission ideas. Joint operations are very important in today's military. Below: CPT Biele tries to work out but he isn't fooling me. Relaxing anyway you could was very important in Iraq.

Passengers in back row of seats on a Blackhawk. LT. Sylvester's glasses cannot hide the thousand yard stare under them. Sometimes the hardest part of the mission was just getting where you had to go. Other times, the mission became just surviving the trip itself. Traveling through Iraq could be like going through Detroit or Philadelphia. You never knew if you would make it.

Bessie Bardot an Australian actress who came to entertain the troops on stage, spends some time entertaining my friends up close.

Below: It is Speedo social time at the pool. This man, an Italian, wore his Speedo all the time at the pool, despite the fact that the lifeguard told him they were not allowed. It was so funny to hear him talk about it with his accent. He would say, "I am at the pool. This is my swimsuit. What is the problem?"

We came up with all sorts of ways to pass the time—trivia contests, Google searches, or reading each other's hometown newspapers. Even having foot races in the middle of the day was better than being bored. In America, you could not fathom sprinting in 110-degree weather while wearing pants and boots, yet that is what we did.

Here I am being silly with United States
Marine Captain Biele. He was one of the
crew that hung out with us at night with
the soldiers from other countries. He is
now stationed somewhere in Virginia.

Above: The two LTs O'Neil and Furlani. Whenever I'm not with him, she seems to be with him. Furlani was my best friend in Iraq, and we are still in contact to this day.

Right: Ukrainians and Italians discuss strategy with good times in their cups as well.

SFC Cardenas U.S. Army catches some sleep while we all stare at him. Sleep was always at a premium. You learn quickly to get it in when you can. If you have a mission or are awakened by an incoming mortar round, it can seem like you can never get enough sleep.

5

VIOLENCE

The remnants of a U.S.-made Ford Explorer after a suicide car bomb attack. This is what a Ford Explorer looks like after a car bomb goes off nearby. All of the plastic and glass is gone; some rubber remains on the tire rims. In this one, everything else burned—including the people. This attack happened in front of me on the highway going into the green zone. I was riding in an Explorer at the time as well, as I did quite often in Baghdad—no extra armor—just an SUV in the city. But it did have a security system, in addition to my M-16 sticking out the window.

This car carried explosives. Incidents and scenes like this make it difficult and downright scary for me to drive down the highways—even in America. It's a fear that you can't understand until you've experienced it, as we did here on the streets of Baghdad.

Dead bodies are the result of indiscriminate killing—from a car bomb in traffic. The Palestine Hotel where foreign journalists stayed is pictured in the background on the right.

Even in black and white, you can clearly see the blood stains on the inside of this commuter bus, following an attack.

Left: Charred bodies—it happens so fast the victims don't even have a chance to move from their seats.

Right: Heat so intense from a car bomb, the human skull is exposed.

Right: A U.S. Army contractor's wallet, left behind after his evacuation.

Far Right: Iraqi Highway Patrol stops some bandits along the road for questioning.

Left: Under UN resolutions these missiles were illegal due to their excessive range capabilities. Does the news care at all? They probably think I staged this photo at a U.S. base anyways.

Right: Apache down! Not a Blackhawk but still like the movie.

Left: Fuel tanker on fire after an attack by an IED. Everyone needed fuel. Sometimes the only way to get it there was by a good ol' tanker. The insurgents knew this as well.

Right: Saddam loyalty tattoo on the arm of a prisoner.

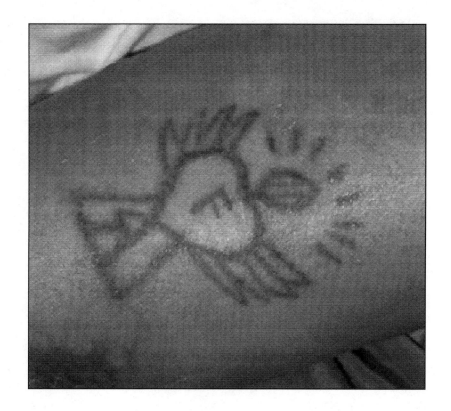

Left: Here soldiers and Iraqis are digging survivors out of the rubble by hand and with whatever else they could find. The rubble was caused when insurgents lured the Iraqi police into a pre-wired apartment building and then set off the explosions as people slept.

Right: An unidentified headless corpse recovered from the river in Baghdad. He was found with his hands still bound behind him (below) by a piece of chain. Savages didn't even give him a chance to fight for his life—they just killed him like the cowards they are.

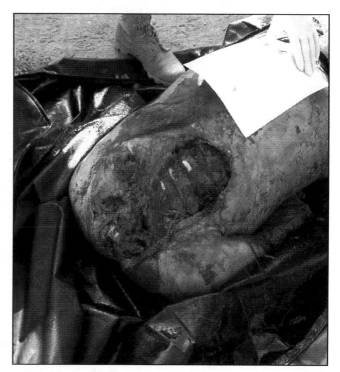

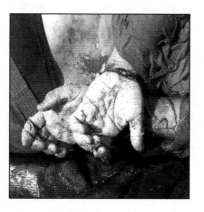

In both photos, a U.S. soldier receives medical attention, including a tourniquet around his upper arm, to stop the flow of blood.

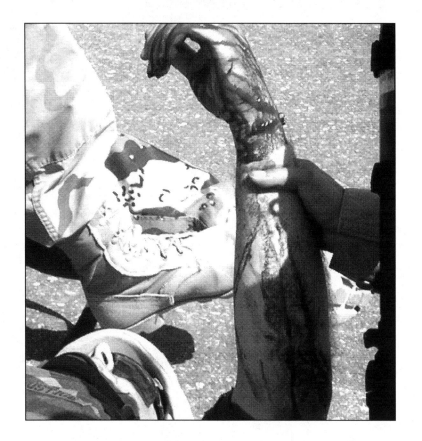

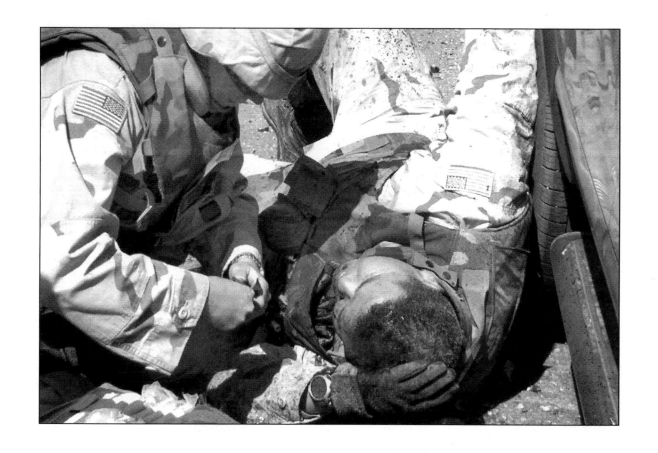

Right: Soldier on blood-stained stairs— Battle of Najaf, 2004.

Far Right: The add-on armored doors were all that was left after this Humvee burned down to the frame. All the armor in the world cannot protect you when it is your time. Life and death in an instant. No political debate, no time, just death.

In both photos,
sleeping marines take
a break from the stress
of battle.

Houston native PFC Ivan Gallegos, a rifleman with Company C, 1st Battalion, 64th Armor Regiment, 2nd Brigade Combat Team, 3rd Infantry Division, pauses for a rest in front of an abandoned building in western Baghdad. Gallegos's platoon found explosive-making materials and homemade explosives during a search of the property, which was subsequently destroyed by an explosive ordnance disposal team. The soldiers, based out of Fort Stewart, GA., operate in western Baghdad as part of the 2nd Brigade Combat Team, 1st Infantry Division. (U.S. Army photo by SPC L.B. Edgar, 7th Mobile Public Affairs Detachment.)

Crestview, FL native PFC Jason Johnson, a rifleman Company C, 1st Battalion, 64th Armor Regiment, 2nd Brigade Combat Team, 3rd Infantry Division, searches the rubble of an abandoned building in western Baghdad. Johnson's platoon found explosive-making materials and homemade explosives during a search of the property, which was subsequently destroyed by an explosive ordnance disposal team. The soldiers, based out of Fort Stewart, GA operate in western Baghdad as part of the 2nd Brigade Combat Team, 1st Infantry Division. (U.S. Army photo by SPC L.B. Edgar, 7th Mobile Public Affairs Detachment.)

An Iraqi National Police officer with the 2nd Battalion, 5th Regiment, 2nd National Police Division, looks through the rubble of an abandoned building in western Baghdad. The National Police searched with Soldiers from Company C, 1st Battalion, 64th Armor Regiment, 2nd Brigade Combat Team, 3rd Infantry Division, and found explosive-making materials and homemade explosives during a search of the property. In both this photo and photo on right, the explosive material was destroyed by an explosive ordinance disposal team. The Soldiers, based out of Fort Stewart, GA., operate in western Baghdad as part of the 2nd Brigade Combat Team, 1st Infantry Division. (U.S. Army photo by SPC L.B. Edgar, 7th Mobile Public Affairs Detachment.)

Explosive-making materials and homemade explosives found by the Soldiers of Company C, 1st Battalion, 64th Armor Regiment, 2nd Brigade Combat Team, 3rd Infantry Division, await disposal following the search of an abandoned building in western Baghdad.

Left: PVT Juri Tikk, a scout with Estonian Platoon 15, which works with Troop B, 1st Squadron, 7th Cavalry Regiment, 1st Brigade Combat Team, 1st Cavalry Division, keeps a watchful eye on the streets in Saba al Bor, a town on the northern outskirts of Baghdad Province, during a search of a predominantly Shia neighborhood. The Estonian soldiers searched abandoned buildings and residents' homes for unauthorized weapons, explosives, and signs of criminal-militia operations. (U.S. Army photo by SPC L.B. Edgar, 7th Mobile Public Affairs Detachment.)

Below: I'm holding up up "dead boxes" from a target practice shooting session in the desert.

BULLSEYE!

CHILDREN

Right: I'm reaching into a bag full of shoes to pass out to Iraqi children.

Far Right: Note the joy and excitement on the faces of these kids, upon receiving something as simple as a pair of shoes. I am no tax-and-spend liberal, yet I cannot look a child in the eye and say tough luck for being born in the wrong place and time.

Left: Just another Iraqi youngster who wants freedom. When I see photos like this, I am reminded of how hard life can be for innocent children.

Right: Iraqi father and daughter pose for the camera during a peaceful moment on the street. Life goes on normally for millions of people living in Iraq. In fact, the majority of Iraq is peaceful on any given day.

I don't think this boy and his friend were related at all. Sometimes it's hard to tell if they just happened to be in the same place at the same time the photo was taken.

 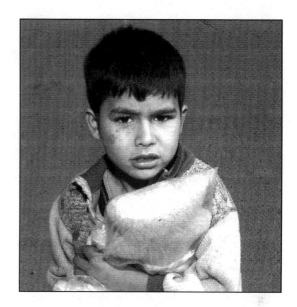

This is most likely the first time this little Iraqi boy has ever received a toy (right).

Left: A framed photograph of a previous meeting is presented to an Iraqi family by my company commander, Captain Snyder.

Right: More happy Kurdish children on the streets in Iraq.

Far Left: Kurdish children with an Italian general in the city of Erbil in Northern Iraq.

Left: Here I am posing with direct descendents of the prophet Abraham inside their ancenstral compound in the city of Ur in southern Iraq. The cities named in the Old Testament are real and, in some cases, still inhabited.

LT Kyle Abruzzese, the fire support officer of Company C, 2nd Battalion, 325th Airborne Infantry Regiment, 2nd Brigade Combat Team, 82nd Airborne Division, hands out contact cards to residents of Ur, a neighborhood in Baghdad's Adhamiyah District. (U.S. Army photo by SPC L.B. Edgar, 7th Mobile Public Affairs Detachment.)

An Iraqi boy speaks with Wadley, Alabama native SFC Kenneth Adams, the 1st Platoon sergeant of Company C, 2nd Battalion, 325th Airborne Infantry Regiment, 2nd Brigade Combat Team, 82nd Airborne Division, in Ur, a neighborhood within Baghdad's Adhamiyah District. The paratroopers went door-to-door to gather information from residents who were being terrorized by criminal militia. (U.S. Army photo by SPC L.B. Edgar, 7th Mobile Public Affairs.)

Valencia, California native Emmanuel Ceballos, the senior medic of Company C, 2nd Battalion, 325th Airborne Infantry Regiment, 2nd Brigade Combat Team, 82nd Airborne Division, pulls security while two Iraqi boys look on in Ur, a neighborhood within Baghdad's Adhamiyah District. (U.S. Army photo by SPC L.B. Edgar, 7th Mobile Public Affairs Detachment.)

...at least these children look happy.

An Iraqi boy finds comfort in the arms of an Iraqi National Police officer with the 2nd Battalion, 5th Regiment, 2nd National Police Division, during a search of the boy's neighborhood in western Baghdad. The National Police paired with soldiers of Company C, 1st Battalion, 64th Armor Regiment, 2nd Brigade Combat Team, 3rd Infantry Division, in discovering bomb-making materials in an abandoned house. (U.S. Army photo by SPC L.B. Edgar, 7th Mobile Public Affairs Detachment.)

An Estonian soldier receives a glass of water from an Iraqi boy as other members of Estonian Platoon 15 take a break in Saba al Bor, a town on the northern outskirts of Baghdad Province, during a search of a predominantly Shia neighborhood. The Estonian soldiers, who work with Troop B, 1st Squadron, 7th Cavalry Regiment, 1st Brigade Combat Team, 1st Cavalry Division, searched abandoned buildings and residents' homes for unauthorized weapons, explosives and signs of criminal-militia operations. (U.S. Army photo by SPC L.B. Edgar, 7th Mobile Public Affairs Detachment.)

Left: An Iraqi boy holds a stuffed animal in Saba al Bor, a town on the northernoutskirts of Baghdad Province, during a search of a predominantly Shia neighborhood. The boy's father spoke with soldiers of Troop B, 1st Squadron, 7th Cavalry Regiment, 1st Brigade Combat Team, 1st Cavalry Division, during a mission to improve security in town. (U.S. Army photo by SPC L.B. Edgar, 7th Mobile Public Affairs Detachment.)

Right: Killeen, Texas, native SGT Nicholas Anderson, 24, the Estonian liaison for Troop B, 1st Squadron, 7th Cavalry Regiment, 1st Brigade Combat Team, 1st Cavalry Division, takes a breather along with an Estonian soldier as a boy looks on in Saba al Bor. The Soldiers searched for unauthorized weapons, explosives and evidence of criminal militias inside residents' homes. (U.S. Army photo by SPC L.B. Edgar, 7th Mobile Public Affairs Detachment.)

CPT Snyder, my company commander, takes time to speak with a young girl—down on her level.

7

HISTORY

The Iraqi people use these beads not only for prayer (similar to Catholic rosary beads), but they claim to have arthritic healing powers.

An excavator at the tombs of Ur. One of the most interesting sites at Ur was an ancient trash dump with a thousand years of broken pottery to be examined. The ancient dump was a great place to pretend you were Indiana Jones on an adventure.

Saddam built a home on this ground, which, based on archeological findings, is thought to be the site of the home of the Prophet Abraham. Saddam had the house built for Pope John Paul II's planned visit to Iraq in 1991, which was cancelled for security reasons. The home included this hole in the ground—the remains of a primitive toilet.

The next generation of Ur.

The tour guide of Ur, whose family has been farming the area for 7,000 years, donates his time to teach visitors about his holy land.

Above: Inside the tour guide's home at Ur, with his father in the background.

Right: I am about 20 meters below the surface, under an ancient archway.

The excavated tombs of Ur, with Ziggurat in the background. The family who lives here says much is still to be discovered under the sands of time in the surrounding area.

Pictographs, like these from Ur, are the oldest known form of writing in the world.

Above and Right: Ur Grandfather and Grandson.

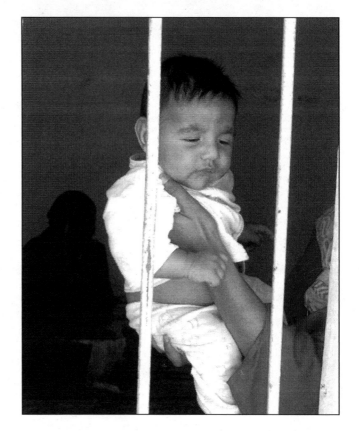

Looking up the steps of the Ziggurat creates an optical illusion of looking down a well. I ran up and down these steps several times. Yankee Stadium in New York was built in 1923 and torn down only decades later. This building is thousands of years old, and these steps are as strong today as they were then. The top of the structure has an altar made of wood where ceremonies were performed for the moon goddess.

ANIMALS

As common at it is to see a squirrel crossing in front of our cars in the U.S. are camels in Iraq, sometimes alone and sometimes in large herds.

Left: While Saddam lives in opulence, his people continue to use donkeys and horses as beasts of burden, the same way they have since before the time of Christ.

Right: Thousand of camels currently roam the deserts of Iraq the same way they have for centuries.

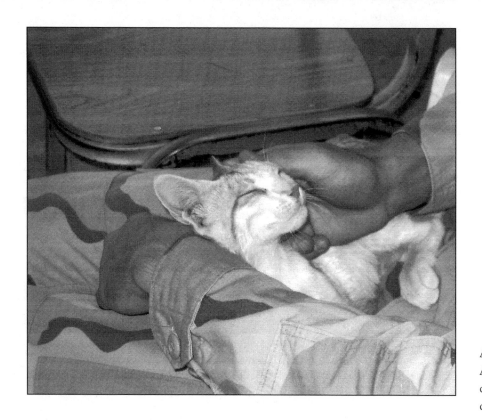

An Iraqi cat and an American soldier— offering a few seconds of solace to one another.

Cats roam the streets at will. There is no spay and neuter program in Iraq. The people don't keep domestic pets like Westerners do. During my stay in Iraq, I never saw a pet in a home—or an animal that even had a name. I did take time to pet this cat myself—a savage little kitty that begged for food on the streets.

It is common to see Iraqi people using donkeys as a means of transportation. The donkey had so much cargo you could hardly see him under the man at all.

THE PEOPLE, THE COUNTRYSIDE & THE CULTURE

9

Local Iraqi man cleaning an unknown object in the street.

September 7th, 2004—the first rain clouds of the year appeared in the sky.

Iraqi asphalt plant right along the highway. This bridge spans the Euphrates River. The checkpoint was manned by Italians. I took friendly fire from this position one night. Murphy's law of combat: friendly fire isn't.

A surveyor collects information from vast desert land. Notice highway in progress in background.

A young Iraqi man
catching a brief
moment of shade.

Iraqi National Police officers speak with an elderly woman during the search of her home in western Baghdad. She and other residents of the neighborhood were later evacuated for their safety when the soldiers and National Police found bomb materials in a nearby abandoned house. (U.S. Army photo by SPC L.B. Edgar, 7th Mobile Public Affairs Detachment)

Two volunteers speak with a local woman concerned for her son being questioned in Saba al Bor, a town on the northern outskirts of Baghdad Province, during a search of a predominantly Shia neighborhood. Soldiers of Troop B, 1st Squadron, 7th Cavalry Regiment, 1st Brigade Combat Team, 1st Cavalry Division, questioned and then released the suspect after determining he was not a wanted man. (U.S. Army photo by Spc. L.B. Edgar, 7th Mobile Public Affairs Detachment.)

This unique road entrance sets nothing less than an ominous mood. This was constructed to celebrate Iraq's victory over Iran in their long-running war.

Right: Interesting road sign.

Center: Iraqi police pose with their commander, Major Ali (3rd from right, top row). He was later killed.

Far Right: Police in the back of one of their trucks.

Iraqi asphalt plant.

Iraqi police station. Notice the wires for generators, internet, and cable, strung all over the building. Along with civil service, infrastructure has a long way to go in Iraq.

This photo was taken
in an area of Iraq safe
enough to dress down
for a moment

COURTROOM SKETCHES FROM THE ABU GHRAIB TRIALS

10

Far Left: Two prosecutors.

Left: Defendant SSG Frederick. A marine corporal that I knew made these pastel sketches of the trial in Iraq. I was able to sit in on the proceedings by agreeing to sharpen her pencils as needed. I was willing to do whatever it took to sit in on a war crime trial, regardless of the outcome.

Right: Prosecutor Major Mike Holley.

Far Right: Defense table, where Gary Meyers, a well-known civilian defense attorney from Washington, D.C., sits with his client SSG Frederick, who was found guilty of several crimes as the non-commissioned officer in charge of a section of the prison where many abuses took place.

11

PROGRESS

CPT Snyder takes time
to speak with Iraqi
children in the streets.

A rare photo of a male soldier with a female Muslim on the street. Iraqi women rarely interact publicly with men in their own society, let alone with a member of U.S. personnel. This photo is very telling of the progress on the street level.

One Australian, two Americans, an Iraqi, and a Canadian—all working together in Iraq. Don't believe the "left" when they say we are going it alone. The proof is in these photos.

A young Iraqi boy shakes hands with MG Walter Natynczyk, Canadian Forces, on loan to America. The photo was taken at the completion of a major highway project.

Iraqi asphalt plant right along the highway. This highway construction project was a major undertaking to provide a paved road all the way from Kuwait to the border with Turkey. Fully 25 percent of US deaths were the result of simple traffic accidents. So road safety for all was important mission for our engineer assets.

These are gold bars that came out of the very palace basement that I sometimes worked out of at Camp Victory—each solid gold bar weighs 2.2 kilograms. While his people suffered, Saddam collected wealth and riches. This pallet was just one example of the hundreds of millions of dollars that Saddam and his loyalists had hidden away from their people and the rest of the world. It was never the sanctions that caused children to starve. It was Saddam himself.

Australian pool, soon to be refurbished and open for business.

The flag of Poland. Every country is proud of its service in Iraq and displays its pride as much as it can. Traveling from an area controlled by one country, to another was really like taking a trip to that place. The language, food, drink, and customs was a whirlwind experience, especially for American soldiers who had never really traveled to another country or served on a joint mission before.

Mission planning takes place wherever you can find a flat area to lay your maps out on.

Wounded Arab fighter receives treatment from American medics with the help of a John Deere Gator tractor! Once the bullets stop, everyone becomes a patient.

Photo collage including *Time* Magazine's Person of the Year issue, honoring "The American Soldier." Ask yourself—shouldn't the soldier be on this cover every year?

Arab prisoners of
all nationalities await
processing.

Above: Saddam with blood on his head. Too bad it wasn't from one of his people getting a chance to beat him! In this photo, Saddam is still wearing flex cuffs on his wrists after being captured.

Top Right: Saddam stroking his beard, like he hasn't a care in the world.

Lower Right: Saddam after a haircut and a shower.

This is a statue in the northern Kurdish City of Erbit. Notice all the children crawling on it to mug for the camera.

In 2005, I went to Crawford, Texas, to show my support of the president and our troops. While there, I met Cindy Sheehan and informed her that while I was saddened by the loss of her son, Casey, she is not any more important than my mom—or anyone else's for that matter. We had a private conversation away from the press, where we just agreed to disagree. Protests in America at any time are appropriate, however any cause can take it too far, and hurt the situation overall.

I hope you've enjoyed the collection of photos, and that it adds to your understanding of the history we have made in Iraq, and the sacrifices involved. Look for my next book, a collection of political satire and Americana, coming in 2009.

Other books by Phil Kiver:
182 Days in Iraq
A Year of Reaction at Home

Order books from www.wordassociation.com, or wherever books are sold.

WA